CAMBRIDGE
UNIVERSITY PRESS

CAMBRIDGE ENGLISH
Language Assessment
Part of the University of Cambridge

CAMBRIDGE

T0343455

# Home FUN booklet 1

Melissa Owen

# Letter to parents

Dear parents,

Welcome to *The Home Fun Booklet*! We hope you will use the activities inside to help your child practise English at home and with their friends.

Your child will bring home this booklet to practise with you what they have learned in class. You don't need to be an English expert to help your child with these activities. All the answers and audio recordings are online at http://www.cambridge.org/funresources . Have fun and keep practising with your child. Try to use the vocabulary here in everyday life and games and don't worry about making mistakes. On pages 7, 11, 15, 19 and 23 you will see this tree:

This tree shows how your child's knowledge will grow and progress through the units. Ask your child to read the 'I can…' sentences in the tree and to think about what they say. They can colour in the leaves green, orange or red when they agree – try to say 'Well done!'

The *Let's have fun!* pages (24-25) feature activities that develop language, mathematical, digital, social, learning and cultural skills useful for modern life. Look for the following signs next to activities in the booklet to show which of these skills your child is developing:

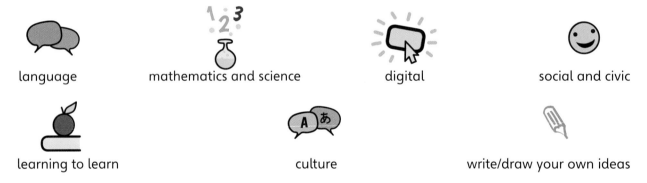

| language | mathematics and science | digital | social and civic |
| --- | --- | --- | --- |

| learning to learn | culture | write/draw your own ideas |
| --- | --- | --- |

The picture dictionary at the end of the booklet (pages 26-31) is for your child to write in through the year. Ask them to write the words they know from all the topics. Make sure they can see they are progressing!

This booklet helps to prepare children for the Cambridge English: Young Learners tests which are a great way to give your child more confidence in English and reward their learning. For more information, please go to: http://www.cambridgeenglish.org/exams/young-learners-english/ .

We hope both you and your child enjoy using this booklet and have fun!

The Cambridge Team

Download the Word FUN World app

# Contents

**Melissa Owen**

# Numbers

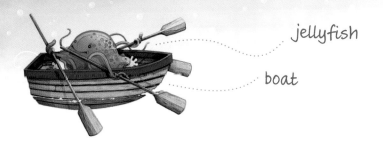

jellyfish

boat

## A  Write the numbers.

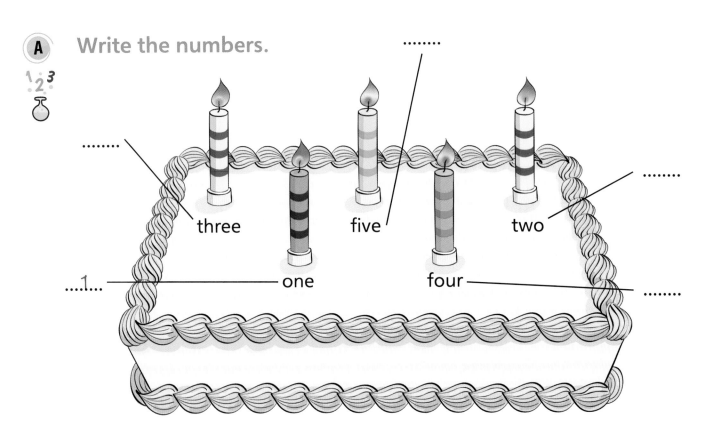

three

five

two

....1....  one

four

## B  Draw lines.

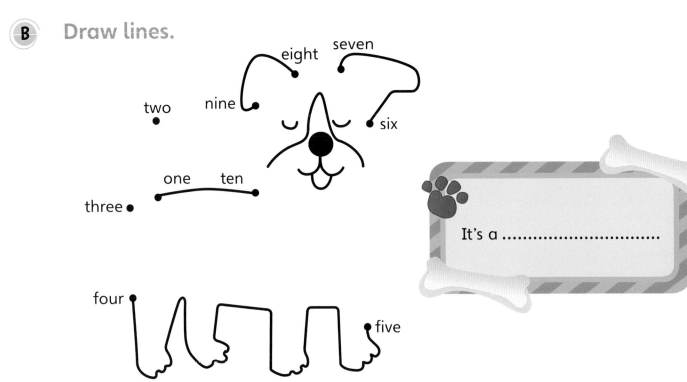

eight    seven

two    nine    six

one    ten

three

four    five

It's a ..............................

**Draw lines.**

1   **4**

2   **6**

3   **1**

4   **7**

5   **8**

6   **5**

7   **3**

8   **9**

9   **2**

10  **10**

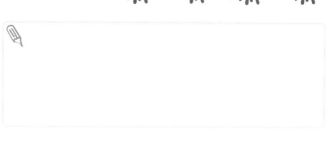

# Toys

**A** Read and draw lines.

**1** I've got a kite.

**2** I've got a bike.

**3** I've got a bat.

**4** I've got a doll.

**5** I've got a guitar.

**B** Look and write.

| green | truck | ~~red~~ | blue | ~~guitar~~ | bat |

**1** I've got a .....*guitar*.......
It's .............*red*.............

**2** I've got a .....................
It's .............................

**3** I've got a .....................
It's .............................

**4** I've got a .....................
It's .............................

6

**C** **Fun at home** Read and colour the answers yellow and green.

What's your name?

How old are you?

My name's Pat.

I'm 8.

Ask your friends and family.

What's your name?
.My. name's. Pat.........
How old are you?
..I'm. 8...............

What's your name?
.My. name's..............
How old are you?
..I'm........................

What's your name?
.My. name's..............
How old are you?
..I'm........................

 I can draw lines from words to pictures.

I can count from 1–10.

I can talk about toys.

I can ask questions.

= 😊

= 😐

= 🙁

# Family

Circle the family words.

grandpa**mum**pencildadpresentblue
greensisterteacherballoonbrother

This is my family.

B Draw lines.

1 This is my mum.

2 This is my sister.

3 This is my brother.

4 This is my dad.

5 This is my grandpa.

**c** Draw and write.

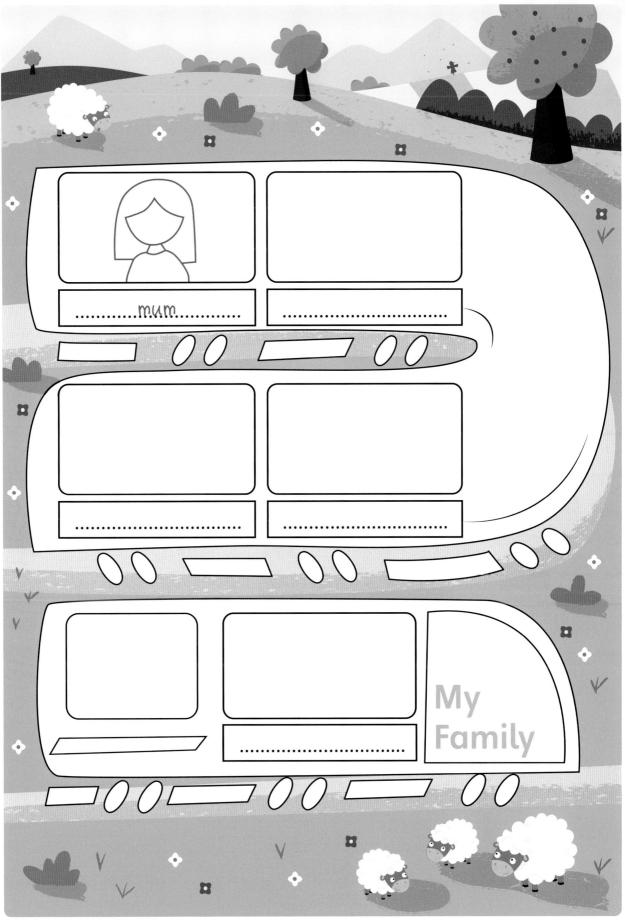

..........mum...........

...........................

...........................          ...........................

...........................

My Family

# School

**A**  Put a tick ( ✓ ) or a cross ( ✗ ) in the box.

**A あ**  **1** This is a poster.  ✗

**4** This is a classroom.  ☐

**2** This is a book.  ☐

**5** This is a bag.  ☐

**3** This is an eraser.  ☐

**B**  Read, colour and write.

|  | Hugo | Me |
|---|---|---|
| school bag | red | ...................... |
| ruler | blue | ...................... |
| pencils | yellow | ...................... |
| crayons | pink | ...................... |
| book | brown | ...................... |

I can write colours.

I can say classroom words.

I can listen and colour.

I know family words.

# Review

**A**  Draw lines.

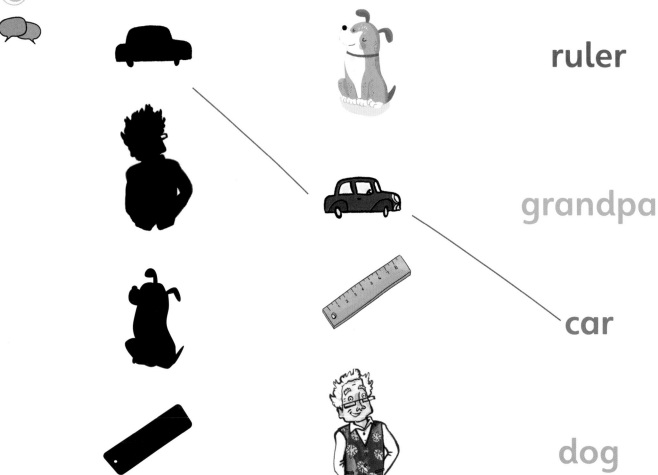

ruler

grandpa

car

dog

**B**  Colour the school words green.
Colour the family words **brown**.
Colour the toy words blue.

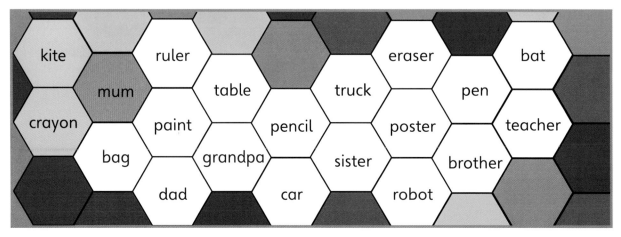

kite  ruler  eraser  bat

mum  table  truck  pen

crayon  paint  pencil  poster  teacher

bag  grandpa  sister  brother

dad  car  robot

**Fun at home** Look and draw lines. Tell your family.

teacher  bag  robot  poster  doll  table  ruler

Where's the ruler?

Here!

# Animals

**A** Look and write.

**1**

o g d
........dog........

e t h p e l a n
.....elephant.....

**2**

i h o p p
....................

m n o e k y
....................

**3**

c o d r i c o l e
....................

d k c u
....................

**4**

....................

....................

**B** Look, read and write.

|  | swim | jump | run | fly |
|---|---|---|---|---|
| monkey | ✗ | ✓ | ✓ | ✗ |
| elephant | ✓ | ✗ | ✓ | ✗ |
| duck | ✓ | ✓ | ✓ | ✓ |
| crocodile | ✓ | ✗ | ✓ | ✗ |

**1**

I can .......jump..........
I can't ........fly........

**3**

I can ......................
I can't ......................

**2**

I can ......................
I can't ......................

**4**

I can ......................
I can't ......................

C **Fun at home** Think of an animal. Play the game.

I am yellow. I can swim. I can fly.

You're a duck!

I can remember school words.

I can talk about animals.

I can write animal words.

I can say what's in a classroom.

# Home

**A** (Circle) the correct answer.

Where's my robot?

**1** The robot is **in** / **under** / **on** the table.

**2** The robot is **next to** / **under** / **on** the armchair.

**3** The robot is **next to** / **in** / **on** the cupboard.

**4** The robot is **next to** / **in** / **under** the computer.

**B** Draw your toy. Write.

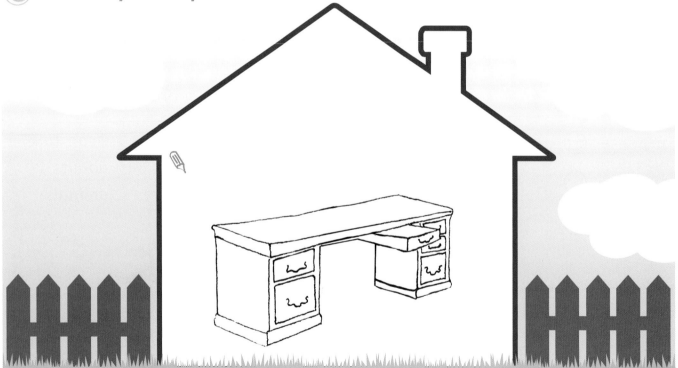

The .................... is .................... the desk.

16

**C** Count and write.

| 5 |  | | | |
|---|---|---|---|---|
| 4 | lamp | | | armchair |
| 3 | lamp | sofa | | armchair |
| 2 | lamp | sofa | table | armchair |
| 1 | lamp | sofa | table | armchair |

How many lamps have I got?

**1** Jill has got five ....lamps.........

**2** Jill has got three ................

**3** Jill has got two ................

**4** Jill has got four ................

**D** What's in your house? Draw and write.

| 5 | | | | |
|---|---|---|---|---|
| 4 | | | | |
| 3 | | | | |
| 2 | | | | |
| 1 | | | | |

How many chairs have you got?

**1** I've got ....................

**2** I've got ....................

**3** I've got ....................

**4** I've got ....................

lamps    sofas    tables    armchairs

# Sports

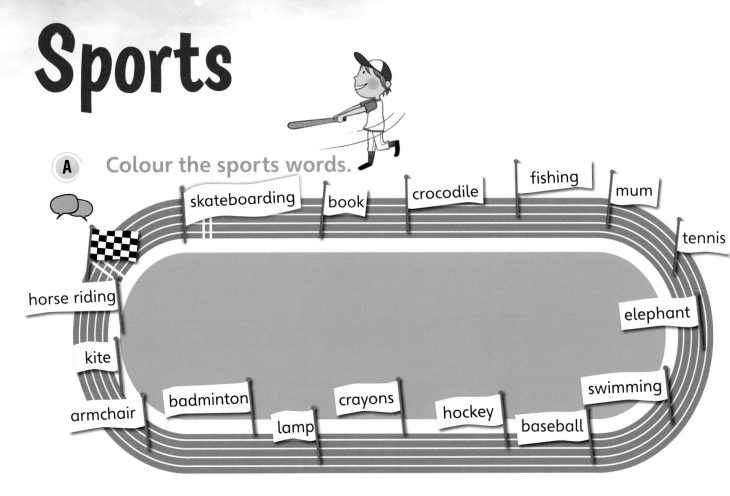

**A** Colour the sports words.

skateboarding   book   crocodile   fishing   mum

tennis

horse riding

elephant

kite

swimming

armchair   badminton   crayons   hockey   baseball

lamp

**B** Look and write.

1 I like *horse riding.*
2 I like ......................
3 I like ......................

1 I like ...*baseball*.....
2 I like ......................
3 I like ......................

1 I like ......................
2 I like ......................
3 I like ......................

**C**  **Listen and draw lines.**

4

**1** ALICE

**2** GRACE

**3** MATT

**4** BEN

✓

◯ I can say the sports I like.

◯ I can write sports words.

◯ I can count things in my house.

◯ I can talk about my home.

= 😊

= 😐

= 🙁

19

# Food

**A** Read and draw lines.

**B** Draw your food and write.

### My shopping list

- grapes
- chicken
- oranges
- carrots
- tomatoes
- chocolate
- apples
- meatballs

I like ...................... and ......................

**Fun at home** Go online and make a spinner. Play the game!

Start

| 6 | 1 |
|---|---|
| 5 | 2 |
| 4 | 3 |

1 2 3 4 5 6 7 8 9 10 11 12 13 14 15 16 17 18 19 20 21 22 23 24 25

Well done!

21

# Review

**A** Read, write and colour.

I can see...

**1** one black ...computer......

**2** two brown ......................

**3** three blue ......................

**4** four purple ......................

**5** five yellow ......................

**B** Where are you? Draw you and your family.

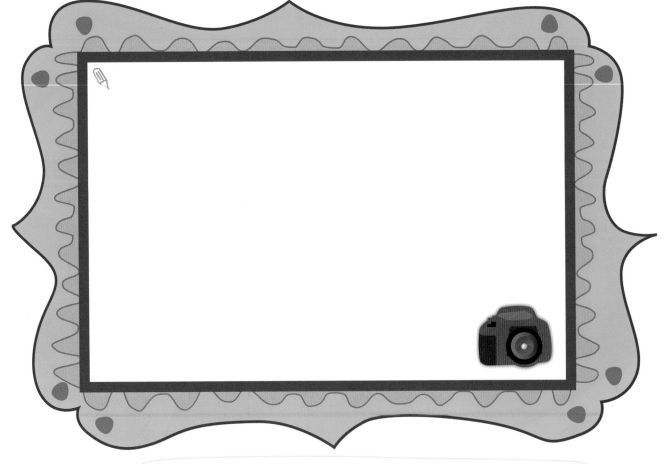

We're at ...........................................................................

**C** 𝐹𝑢𝑛 𝑎𝑡 𝑕𝑜𝑚𝑒 **Write five words. Play the game!**

Five words!
Well done!

|   | A | B | C | D |
|---|---|---|---|---|
| 1 |   |   |   |   |
| 2 |   |   |   |   |
| 3 | apple |   |   |   |
| 4 |   |   |   |   |

1D?

No, sorry. Put a cross.

3A?

Yes, it's apple.
A-P-P-L-E.

= ☺

= 😐

= ☹

I can play a game.

I can say
the food
I like.

I can talk
about food.

I know words
for places.

# Let's have fun!

**A** **Fun at home** Ask your friend three questions. Make a video.

**B** Where can you help? Draw lines.

**shops**

**school**

**home**

**park**

24

**C** Take photos of three signs you see in English.

**D** What's the first letter? Write and draw the toys.

**1**

bike | apple | lamp | lamp

B | A | L | L

**2**

**3**

**4**

# Picture dictionary

......bear......

## The body and the face

......arm...... ..................... ..................... ..................... .....................

..................... ..................... ..................... .....................

## Clothes

......bag...... ..................... ..................... ..................... .....................

..................... ..................... ..................... ..................... .....................

..................... ..................... ..................... ..................... ..................... .....................

## Colours

..................... ..................... .....................

......black...... ..................... .....................

..................... ..................... .....................

27

## Family and friends

......baby...... ..................

.................. ..................

..................

## Food and drink

 .....apple..... .................. .................. ..................

.................. .................. .................. .................. ..................

.................. .................. .................. .................. ..................

.................. .................. .................. ..................

.................. .................. .................. ..................

.................. .................. .................. ..................

..armchair..

.......................

.......................

.......................

.......................

.......................

.......................

.......................

.......................

.......................

.......................

.......................

.......................

.......................

.......................

.......................

.......................

.......................

.......................

.......................

.......................

.......................

.......................

.......................

.......................

.......................

.......................

.......................

## Places

.....park.....

.......................

.......................

.......................

.......................

## School

2×2=

....board....

.............

.............

.............

.............

.............

.............

.............

.............

.............

.............

.............

.............

.............

.............

.............

.............

.............

.............

.............

.............

## Sports and leisure

badminton

.............

.............

.............

.............

.............

.............

.............

.............

.............

.............

.............

.............

.............

.............

.............

.............

.............

.............

.............

.............

.............

.............

.............

.............

.............

.............

.............

.............

## Time

.....birthday.....          ...................          ...................

## Toys

.....alien.....          ...................          ...................          ...................          ...................

...................          ...................          ...................          ...................

## Transport

.....boat.....          ...................          ...................          ...................          ...................

...................          ...................          ...................          ...................

## The world around us

.....sea.....          ...................          ...................

## Acknowledgements

The author would like to send her love and thanks to her family.

The author and publisher would like to thank the ELT professionals who commented on the material at different stages of development: Karen Elliott, Spain; Mark Manning, Spain; Alice Soydas, Turkey.

Design and typeset by Wild Apple Design.

Cover design and header artwork by Chris Saunders (Astound).

Audio production by Hart McLeod, Cambridge.

The authors and publishers acknowledge the following sources of copyright material and are grateful for the permissions granted. While every effort has been made, it has not always been possible to identify the sources of all the material used, or to trace all copyright holders. If any omissions are brought to our notice, we will be happy to include the appropriate acknowledgements on reprinting.

**The publishers are grateful to the following for permission to reproduce copyright photographs and material:**

Key: BL = Below Left, BR = Below Right, CL = Centre Left, CR = Centre Right, T = Top, TC = Top Centre, TL = Top Left.

p. 24 (T): AzmanL/iStock/Getty Images Plus/Getty Images; p. 24 (CL): Michael H/Photodisc/Getty Images; p. 24 (BL): Steve Debenport/E+/Getty Images; p. 24 (CR): Geri Lavrov/Photographer's Choice/Getty Images; p. 24 (BR): Moof/Cultura/Getty Images; p. 25 (TL): Rafael Elias/Moment/Getty Images; p. 25 (TC): JGI/Jamie Grill/Blend Images/Getty Images; p. 25 (bike): Philip Gatward/Dorling Kindersley/Getty Images; p. 25 (apple): Dorling Kindersley/Dorling Kindersley/Getty Images; p. 25 (lamp): Andy Crawford/Dorling Kindersley/Getty Images; p. 25 (ball): Dorling Kindersley/Dorling Kindersley/Getty Images; p. 25 (ice): Douglas Johns/StockFood Creative/Getty Images; p. 25 (kiwi): Sally Williams Photography/Photolibrary/Getty Images; p. 25 (elephant): Dave King/Dorling Kindersley/Getty Images; p. 25 (tennis): Highwaystarz-Photography/iStock/Getty Images Plus/Getty Images; p. 25 (egg): Alain Caste/StockFood Creative/Getty Images; p. 25 (rug): DEA/G. CIGOLINI/De Agostini Picture Library/Getty Images; p. 25 (orange): David Marsden/Photolibrary/Getty Images; p. 25 (television): tiridifilm/E+/Getty Images.

**The authors and publishers are grateful to the following illustrators:**

T = Top, B = Below, L = Left, R = Right, C = Centre

Laetitia Aynie (Sylvie Poggio Artists Agency) pp. 20, 21 and 28 (chocolate), 28 (sweets); Judy Brown (Beehive Illustration) pp. 4 (T), 26 (cat); David Banks pp. 26 (bird), 28 (lemon), 29 (radio), 31 (shell); Joanna Boccardo pp. 28 (rice), 31 (morning, night); Sasha Ediger pp. 26 (bee); Andrew Elkerton (Sylvie Poggio Artists Agency) pp. 14 (T, B), 15 (T), 26 (bear, duck, giraffe, jellyfish, monkey, zebra), 27 (face), 28 (banana), 29 (box, flower, window), 31 (boat); Chris Embleton-Hall (Advocate Art) pp. 29 (bedroom, zoo), 30 (rubber); Chabe Escalante pp. 31 (tablet, train); Clive Goodyer pp. 27 (smile, watch), 29 (street), 30 (mouse, kick), 31 (truck); Dean Gray (Advocate Art) pp. 9, 19 (map); Andrew Hamilton pp. 19 (football), 21 (fruit), 26 (horse), 27 (dress, glasses, handbag, hat, jacket, jeans, shirt, shoe, skirt, sock, trousers), 29 (garden), 30 (keyboard), 31 (helicopter, plane); Kelly Kennedy (Sylvie Poggio Artists Agency) pp. 5 (hat), 6, 7, 10 (book), 11 (book, pencil), 12 (car), 21 (chips, pear), 26 (frog, lizard), 27 (nose), 28 (chips, pear), 29 (table, tree, park, shop), 30 (book, painting, paper, pencil, school, badminton, baseball, basketball, bat, bike, draw, football, guitar, hockey, kite, piano, read, sing), 31 (ball, doll, monster, robot, teddy bear, car, motorbike); Nigel Kitching pp. 10 (B), 27 (body and face), 30 (board); Marta Alvarez Miguens (Astound) pp. 18, 19 (children, swimming, tennis, skateboard), 22 (skateboard), 23 (Alice), 29 (playground), 30 (beach, fishing, skateboard, tennis racket); Dani Padron (Advocate Art) pp. 10, 11 (boy, bus, classroom, crayons, pen), 12 (ruler), 13 (classroom), 27 (bag, hat), 29 (computer), 30 (classroom, crayons, pen, poster, ruler, teacher), 31 (bus); Bill Piggins pp. 28 (milk), 29 (camera); Nina de Polonia (Advocate Art) pp. 21 (egg), 26 (polar bear), 28 (burger); David Pratt pp.28 (coconut); Pip Sampson pp. 22 (room), 26 (chicken, cow, crocodile, elephant, goat, sheep), 28 (egg, fish, sausage, water), 29 (bath, bathroom, dining room, kitchen, mat, mirror, picture), 30 (bookcase), 31 (ship); Anthony Rule pp. 12 (juice); Chris Saunders (Astound) p. 1, house, jellyfish and tree images throughout; Melanie Sharp (Sylvie Poggio Artists Agency) pp. 8, 11 (paints), 12 (grandpa), 13 (Kim and brother), 14 (jump, run, swim), 15 (spider), 21 (apple), 26 (spider), 28 (brother, dad, grandpa, mum, sister, cake, chicken, ice cream, lemonade), 29 (clock, door, wall), 30 (bounce, catch, jump, run, table tennis, throw), 31 (birthday, alien, balloon, game, sun); Harriet Stanes (NB Illustration) pp. 16, 17, 22 (T), 28 (grandma), 29 (armchair, bed, desk, house, lamp, living room, sofa, TV); Jo Taylor (Sylvie Poggio Artists Agency) pp. 28 (baby, bread, onion, pea, pineapple); Alex Willmore (Astound) pp. 4 (dog), 5 (ball, children, dog, shoe, phone), 12 (dog), 14 (dog), 15 (Ben), 22 (shoe), 26 (dog), 27 (boot), 29 (phone); Sue Woollatt (GI Illustration) pp. 26 (hippo, tiger), 28 (watermelon), 31 (sea); Gaby Zermeño pp. 20, 21, 22 (pie), 23, 26 (donkey, fish, mouse, snake), 27 (shorts, T-shirt), 28 (apple, carrot, grapes, meatballs, orange, pie, potato, tomato).